Humphrey's Book of Summer Fun

Praise for *The World According to Humphrey*:

'A charming, feel-good tale.' *Irish Times*

'A breezy, well-crafted first novel. Humphrey's matter-of-fact, table-level view of the world is alternately silly and profound and Birney captures his unique blend of innocence and earnestness from the start.' *Publisher's Weekly*

Praise for *Friendship According to Humphrey*:

'An effective exploration of the joys and pains of making and keeping friends, which will strike a chord with many children.' *Daily Telegraph*

Praise for *Trouble According to Humphrey*:

'Children fall for Humphrey, and you can't beat him for feelgood life lessons.' *Sunday Times*

Humphrey's Summer Fun

Betty G. Birney worked at Disneyland and the Disney Studios, has written many children's television shows and is the author of over forty books, including the bestselling *The World According to Humphrey*, which won the Richard and Judy Children's Book Club Award, *Friendship According to Humphrey*, *Trouble According to Humphrey*, *Surprises According to Humphrey*, *More Adventures According to Humphrey*, *Holidays According to Humphrey*, *School According to Humphrey*, *Mysteries According to Humphrey* and *Christmas According to Humphrey*, and seven books in the Humphrey's Tiny Tales series. Her work has won many awards, including an Emmy and three Humanitas Prizes. She lives in America with her husband.

Humphrey's Book of Summer Fun

Betty G. Birney

Compiled by Amanda Li

ff

faber and faber

First published in 2013
by Faber and Faber Limited
Bloomsbury House, 74-77 Great Russell Street
London WC1B 3DA

Printed and bound by CPI Group (UK) Ltd, Croydon, CR0 4YY

Graphic design by Patrick Tate

A CIP record for this book
is available from the British Library

978-0-571-28245-6

2 4 6 8 10 9 7 5 3 1

Summer's here!

When the school year comes to an end, it's time to leave the building, enjoy the sunshine and have **FUN-FUN-FUN**. It's holiday time!

Find out what all my friends from Longfellow School like to do over the summer by completing this little word puzzle that I wrote in my notebook.

Fill in one letter on each line to make two new words. The missing letter will be the last letter of the first word and the first letter of the second word, e.g.

OA **R** OCK

PEA ☐ AT
FAC ☐ ASY
BEL ☐ OVE
SE ☐ PE
BO ☐ -RAY

Rocking Reports

At the end of the school year, Mrs Brisbane gave Og and me our very own school reports. I'm delighted to say we both got unsqueakably straight As! Do you know what our best subjects were? See if you can fill in the missing letters.

Og the Frog
End of Year Report

W_ter Skills	**A**
L_ud N_ise Making	**A**
Spl_s_ing	**A**
Being Very Gr__n	**A**

Humphrey the Hamster
End of Year Report

Wh ee l Spi nn ing　**A**

. . . .

Hamster B _ ll R _ lling　**A**

. . . .

Squ _ _ king　**A**

. . . .

H _ lping Your Fr _ _ nds　**A**

. . . .

well done!

Humphrey's Noises

Longfellow School can be quite a noisy place, sometimes! When I was taken out of school for the summer, I missed some of those noises at first. Still, there was always the familiar **SCREECH** of my wheel going round and round!

Can you remember some of these school sounds and match up them up to who or what is making them? Just draw lines between them.

1. **Boing!**

2. **Giggle!**

3. **Tick-tock**

4 **R-r-ring!**

5. **Creak!**

6. **Squeak!**

7. **Rattle-rattle-rattle!**

Design a Pencil Top

Nobody knows that I have a lock-that-doesn't-lock on my cage door! One time I secretly got out and explored Garth's desk. He had a cup full of wonderful pencils: a smiling monkey, a shining star, an orange pumpkin head, even a rocket! I was impressed!

Can you design some creative pencil tops? Maybe a frog – or a hamster?

Humphrey's Frog Jokes

BOING! There's one creature I can always rely on – that's my friend Og the frog. He doesn't say much, but I know he has a great sense of humour underneath that green skin of his. These jokes are for you, Og!

Which year do frogs like best of all?
A Leap Year!

How did the frog feel when he broke his leg?
Unhoppy.

What do frogs like to eat in restaurants?
French flies.

What goes dot-dot-croak, dot-dash-croak?
Morse toad!

What do you say when you meet a toad?
'Wart's new?'

Og's Pond Maze

My pal Og loves to splash around in water! He wants to jump into this lovely cool pond – can you find the way there for him?

On the way, Og's going to catch some crunchy crickets for a snack. How many will he eat up on his journey?

START

FINISH

Og will eat ___ crunchy crickets!

Finish the Camp Song

One of the best things about being at Camp Happy Hollow for the summer was watching everyone I know having so much fun together. Most nights they sang silly camp songs while Ms Mac played the bongos – I even squeaked along too!

Do you know any of these great camp songs – and can you fill in the missing words?

1. **Do your _____ hang low?**

2. **There's a _____ in my bucket.**

3. **Row, row, row your _____.**

4. **Ten _____ bottles.**

5. **She'll be coming round the _____.**

6. **My Bonnie lies over the _____.**

squeak! squeak!

Dot-to-dot Musical Instrument

Join the dots to find something I heard being played a lot at Camp Happy Hollow. My friend Garth has one too – I think it sounds wonderful!

Outdoor Skills Wordsearch

All my friends at Camp Happy Hollow had such a
GREAT-GREAT-GREAT time doing different outdoor
activities every day. I loved watching them while I was
spinning on my wheel – that's my favourite activity!

Can you find six outdoor activities in this active wordsearch? They might be up, down, across or diagonal.

CANOEING • SWIMMING • ARCHERY
VOLLEYBALL • SOFTBALL • HIKING

V	E	H	G	M	O	I	N	G
O	C	G	N	I	K	I	H	S
L	K	A	R	C	H	E	R	Y
L	S	O	N	M	M	G	C	B
E	O	H	S	O	L	I	N	G
Y	K	V	R	C	E	B	A	R
B	S	W	I	M	M	I	N	G
A	R	C	N	E	L	S	N	C
L	N	O	G	B	A	V	L	G
L	L	A	B	T	F	O	S	R

Humphrey's Stickers

At Camp Happy Hollow, Ms Mac found some fun
stickers – and I sneaked out of my cage to stick them
in some of my friends' books! I think it made Gail and
Brad **HAPPY–HAPPY–HAPPY** to find them the next day.
Here are some of the camp stickers:

Would you like to design your own unsqueakably super
sticker? Think of a fun and happy phrase, then draw a
picture to go with it.

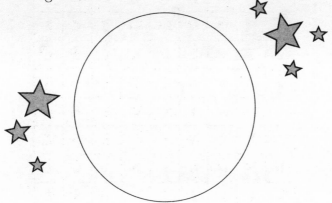

Humphrey's Secret Message

At Camp Happy Hollow we took care of an injured creature, who soon got better and returned to the wild. We even gave her a name – Lovey!

Do you remember what kind of creature Lovey was? Cross out all the letters that appear twice below. Unscramble the remaining letters to find out.

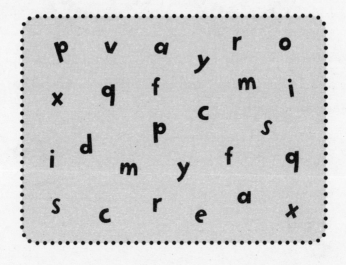

Lovey was a _____ .

Creature Camp

I wasn't the only animal being looked after at Camp Happy Hollow. There were creatures in the Nature Centre too, as well as an old friend of mine. Can you identify each animal? To help you, I've given you a fact about each one.

Flap-flap!　　*Squeak-squeak!*　　*Boing!*

1. Goldenrod has four legs, a long tail and likes to squeak. Goldenrod is a _ _ _ _ _.

2. Lovey was injured at first but ended up flying high! Lovey is a _ _ _ _.

3. Jake has scaly skin and eats bugs, worms, frogs and – eek – small rodents. Jake is a _ _ _ _ _.

4. Og eats crickets and loves the water. Og is a _ _ _ _.

5. Humphrey is a pet who loves helping his friends. Humphrey is a _ _ _ _ _ _ _.

Scritch-scritch-scritch!　　*Hiss-s-s!*

MOUSE • DOVE • SNAKE • FROG • HAMSTER

Humphrey's Secret Message

On the night we went to Haunted Hollow, Hap told us all a scary story about the crazy person who haunts the Hollow. Were we afraid? **YES-YES-YES!**

Do you want to know what they call him? Then cross out all the letters that appear twice below. Unscramble the remaining letters to find out his name.

The scary haunter is called the _____ !

Humphrey's Camping Song

I'll never forget the tuneful camp song that all the children sang at Camp Happy Hollow. Though I did change the words just a tiny bit.

Here's my special version of the song. Can you fill in the missing words?

Happy Hollow - a place close to my _ _ _ _ _ .

Happy Hollow - I _ _ _ _ _ it from the start.

Every day I _ _ _ _ up with so much to do,

Having fun with _ _ and Bunny Foo Foo.

I'll remember for ever my new _ _ _ _ _ _ Goldenrod,

Lovey, too, but Jake is rather _ _ _ .

Though I don't know where I'll be in days that _ _ _ _ _ _ ,

I'll remember _ _ _ _ _ days at Happy Hollow.

```
Happy      woke      follow     loved

odd        heart      Og        friend
```

Which Snake is Jake?

I was more than a little nervous when I discovered that Jake, one of the pets at the Happy Hollow Nature Centre, was a snake!

Would you like to know what kind of snake Jake was? Fill in one letter on each line to make two new words. The missing letter will be the last letter of the first word and the first letter of the second word, e.g.

OA **R** OCK

You will find the answer in the vertical box.

SON		REEN
FLE		NT
ROA		IBBON
BOA		EA
CHEES		GG
TIGE		IVER

This type of snake usually has three stripes running all the way down its back.

Design a Tie

Mr Morales, our headteacher, wears such **FUN-FUN-FUN** ties! They are always brightly coloured, with eye-catching pictures or designs all over them. At summer camp I noticed that he was wearing a tie covered in tiny cars!

Can you design Mr Morales a great tie for the summer months? What kind of summery design will you create?

Humphrey's
Secret Code

Shhh!

A ☀   J ✏   S 🧹

B 🌙   K 🖌   T 🎁

C ⭐   L 🍎   U 🐸

D 🍃   M 🍌   V 🌳

E 🌼   N 🍪   W 🎡

F 🤍   O 🥕   X 🔒

G 🦋   P ⛵   Y 🧀

H 🌈   Q ⚾   Z 🍐

I 📖   R 🎸

I'm very good at keeping secrets – and I love secret codes. In my little notebook I've been making up a code using pictures of summery things.

I've written you a message about some other favourite things of mine. Find out what they are by writing each letter in the space as you find it.

___ ___   ___ ___ ___ ___

___ ___ ___ ___ ___ ___ ___ ___

___ ___ ___ ___ ___ ___ ___

Humphrey's Holiday Jokes

As you know, 'Hamsterdam' is my favourite holiday destination. But where do other creatures like to go?

Where do bees like to go on holiday?
Stingapore.

Where do birds like to go on holiday?
The Canary Islands.

Where do cows like to go on holiday?
Moo York.

Where do T-Rexes like to go on holiday?
The dino-shore.

Where do pencils like to go on holiday?
Pencil-vania.

Humphrey's Word Wheel

JOY-JOY-JOY! I just love spinning around on my wheel! It's wheely fun! And great exercise, too.

I've made up a great word puzzle for you, all about my hamster wheel. If you can work it out, you will read a message from me. All you have to do is start at the circled L, then go round the wheel, writing down *every other* letter in the spaces below. (First, L, then E, and so on.) You will go around the wheel twice.

Humphrey's message: ____'__ __ _____ _____!

Fur or Feathers?

All my friends at Longfellow School love to hold me and stroke my soft, golden fur. If they're gentle, I **LOVE-LOVE-LOVE** it too!

But not all animals have fur, as I discovered from my days at Pet-O-Rama, the local pet shop. Some have scales or shells, others feathers or even quills.

Below are the names of six feathered birds and six furry mammals. Can you tell them apart and circle the six birds?

Meerkat

Quail

Kiwi

Gerbil

Albatross

Ocelot

Heron

Ferret

Kestrel

Yak

Falcon

Sloth

Humphrey's Trivia Bee

Mrs Brisbane once did a great quiz for everyone in Room 26 called a Trivia Bee. I think trivia means 'little things that are fun to know' – a bit like me!

I've devised a little quiz of my own – would you like to try it and see how much trivia you know?

1. **Which animal has the largest eyes in the world?**

2. **How many eggs would you get if you asked for half a dozen?**

3. **What are baby goats called?**

4. **Which colour do you get if you mix red and blue?**

5. **What is the name of Peter Pan's pirate enemy?**

6. **How many horns did the Triceratops dinosaur have?**

7. **From which tree do we get conkers?**

8. **How many sides does a hexagon have?**

9. **Which creature has ears on its legs?**

10. **Which fairytale character's nose grew long if he told a lie?**

11. **On which part of the body are the triceps found?**

12. **Which of these is not a type of hamster?**
    a. **Golden**
    b. **Syrian**
    c. **French**
    d. **Chinese**

Hot or Cold?

Did you know that Golden Hamsters, like me, originally come from the desert? That's why I prefer warm days to snowy ones!

Take a look at all these creatures. Can you decide which ones come from hot and which ones come from cold places? Colour in the correct box.

Camel

| Hot |
| Cold |

Kangaroo

| Hot |
| Cold |

Walrus

| Hot |
| Cold |

Polar Bear

Hot
Cold

Ostrich

Hot
Cold

Penguin

Hot
Cold

Lizard

Hot
Cold

Hyena

Hot
Cold

Humphrey's Ice-cream Wordsnake

I noticed that in the summer people (especially children) seem to eat a lot of ice-cream. I haven't tried it myself – I prefer raw vegetables and fruit – but apparently it's **YUM-YUM-YUMMY!** And it comes in many different flavours.

Can you find all these ice-cream flavours in the wordsnake opposite?

Use a pencil to draw a continuous line through the names in the grid (in the same order as the list below). The line will snake up and down, backwards and forwards, but never diagonally.

VANILLA
CHOCOLATE
STRAWBERRY
MINT
TOFFEE
MANGO
COFFEE
BANANA
COCONUT

V	A	N	I	U	T
O	C	O	L	N	O
L	A	H	L	O	C
E	T	C	A	C	A
S	T	R	N	A	N
B	W	A	A	B	E
E	R	O	C	O	E
Y	R	G	N	F	F
M	T	T	A	M	E
I	N	O	F	F	E

Summer Fair Sayings

For the school summer fair, my friends made up sayings about Room 26. They were **GREAT-GREAT-GREAT!** Can you complete the missing words?

Humphrey-Humphrey, Og-Og!
We've got a hamster and a _____ !

BOING-BOING, SQUEAK-SQUEAK
Humphrey and Og —
hear them _____ !

Humphrey and Og are so much fun,
They make our classroom number ____ !

The greatest pets of Longfellow school,
Humphrey and Og are super-_____ !

Face-Painting Fun

Speak-Up-Sayeh had her face painted like a tiger at the school summer fair – she looked **GRRR-EAT!**

If you get some coloured pens, you can do some face painting too. Make this little girl's face into an animal, just like Sayeh. Perhaps a butterfly, a zebra, a frog – or maybe a hamster?

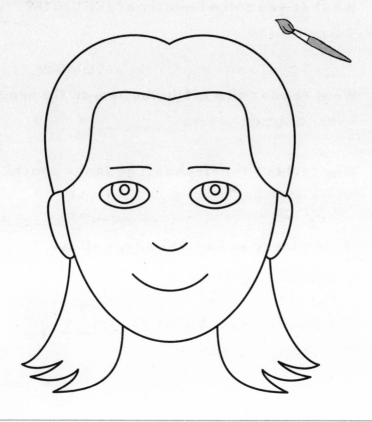

Humphrey's Holiday Jokes

Most humans love going to the beach. But as hamsters should **NEVER-NEVER-NEVER** get wet, I try to avoid the sea!

What do you call a hamster at the beach?
Sandy Claws.

What do you call a witch who lives on the beach?
A sandwitch.

Why couldn't the elephants go to the beach?
They only had one pair of trunks.

What's black and white and red all over?
A sunburnt zebra.

Why did the beach blush?
Because the seaweed!

Dot-to-Dot Beach Fun

Join the dots to find something bright and bouncy. Both humans and animals **LOVE-LOVE-LOVE** to play with it!

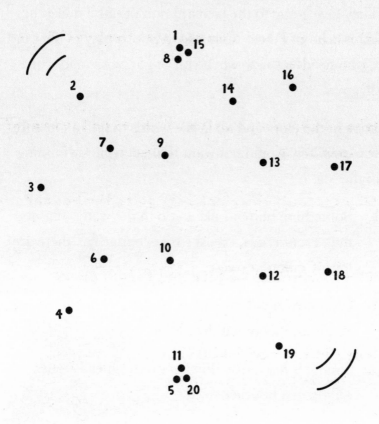

Humphrey's Seaside Word Grid

Og and I are **VERY-VERY-VERY** different. He loves splashing around in water while I'm not too keen on getting wet. But humans seem to be more like Og. They love going to the beach. I don't think I'd like the sea much but I'd certainly like to have a play in the sand – who needs a spade when you've got paws made for digging?

Look at the clues and fill in the words to find a creature you definitely would not want to meet while swimming in the sea!

1. Something humans like to do in the water (but not me). Front crawl, breast stroke, butterfly – there are lots of different styles.

2. It's sandy or pebbly, and if you're looking at the sea, you're probably standing on it.

3. Sailing is fun if you don't get wet! Once I went sailing in a hamster-sized _ _ _ _.

4. This sea creature has pincers and a hard shell. I am a little scared of it!

5. Children seem to love exploring these with a net and a bucket. They often find small creatures, like starfish, left behind from the sea.

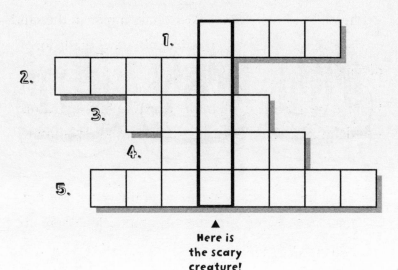

▲
Here is
the scary
creature!

Party Odd One Out

I pawsitively love parties! Summer parties, surprise parties, birthday parties – I just love watching everyone enjoying themselves and having fun.

Take a close look at these great party items. Can you circle one picture in each set of three that is the odd one out?

1.

A   B   C

2.

A   B   C

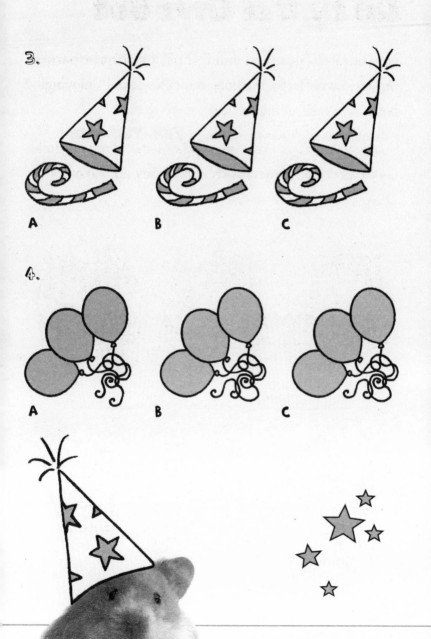

Design a Cupcake

For my birthday, my friends from Room 26 made me
the most wonderful birthday cupcake. It not only looked
fantastic, it was made of nuts, seeds and
raisins – all my favourite things. **YUM-YUM-YUM**!

Can you create some beautiful birthday cupcakes too?
Draw your designs on the paper cases.

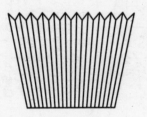

Humphrey's Park Wordsearch

Do you like playing in the park? When the class created the town of Humphreyville, I got to explore – and found a miniature Humphrey-sized park! It was **SO-SO-SO** fun! Can you find six fun things to do in the park in the wordsearch below?

SWING · SLIDE · ROUNDABOUT
SAND PIT · SEE-SAW · MONKEY BARS

M	O	N	K	E	Y	B	A	R	S
S	P	S	E	E	S	A	W	O	M
W	A	F	W	K	U	L	G	U	W
I	U	N	C	I	A	W	N	N	I
N	E	C	D	G	K	B	E	D	G
G	E	B	T	P	F	D	K	A	P
D	N	M	E	E	I	W	H	B	M
B	S	P	U	L	J	T	I	O	B
I	D	N	S	G	A	W	M	U	U
O	U	T	M	W	K	S	K	T	A

Humphrey's Holiday Jokes

If I saw an alligator on holiday, I'd make it snappy and get out of there!

Where can you find alligators on the beach?

In a croc-pool.

What did the ghost send home from his holiday?

Ghostcards.

What folds up and goes 'Quack, Quack'?

A duck-chair.

What's brown, hairy and wears sunglasses?

A coconut on holiday.

How did the film star keep cool on the beach?

She was surrounded by fans.

Ferris Wheel Match Up

It's **FUN-FUN-FUN** to spin round on my hamster wheel. I've never been on a Big Wheel at a funfair but I'm pretty sure I'd love that too!

Look at all these exciting funfair rides. Can you match up the two halves of each name?

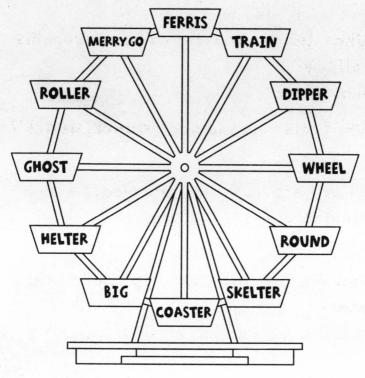

Summer Picture Puzzler

I've made up a puzzle in my little notebook just for you. All these summery things fit into the grid opposite – but where?

Look at the pictures, then write the words in the correct spaces. I've already put in two letters to help you! Just draw lines between them.

Humphrey's Secret Code

Shhh!

A ☀
B 🌙
C ⭐
D 🍃
E 🌸
F 🤍
G 🦋
H 🌈
I 📖

J ✏
K 🖌
L 🍎
M 🍌
N 🍪
O 🥕
P ⛵
Q ⚾
R 🎸

S 🧹
T 🎁
U 🐸
V 🌳
W 🎡
X 🔒
Y 🧀
Z 🍐

I'm having so much fun making up secret codes in my notebook that I thought I'd write you another message. Would you like to know what it is?

Find out by writing each letter in the space as you find it.

___ ___ ___ ___ ___ ___ ' ___

___ ___ ___ ___ ___ ___

___ ___ ___ ___ ___ ___ !

Humphrey Around the World

When Ms Mac went to Brazil, I really missed her. I know Mrs Brisbane misses her son too, now that he lives in Japan. But we both love seeing them when they visit and hearing about all the exciting places they've seen!

On the luggage tags below are five famous cities of the world. But they're all mixed up. Can you unscramble them and write their names underneath the tag?

1.

_ _ _

_ _ _ _

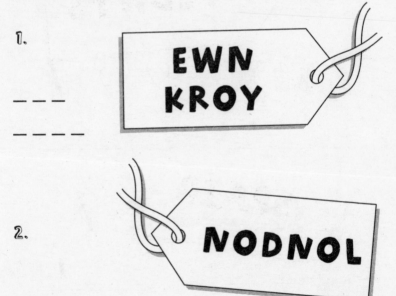

2.

_ _ _ _ _ _

3.

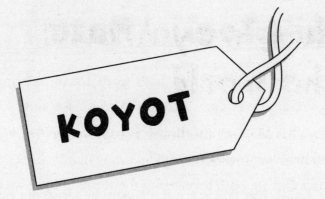

KOYOT

_ _ _ _ _

4.

YEDNYS

_ _ _ _ _ _

5.

SPAIR

_ _ _ _ _

Aki's Rockin' Maze

When Mrs Brisbane came back from Tokyo, she brought a new friend with her – Rockin' Aki! Aki is a tiny hamster with crazy fur that rolls around inside a ball. I think he's unsqueakably cute!

But, unlike me, Aki is just a toy. And he'll run out of batteries soon if he can't get new ones. Can you help him get to the batteries by finding his way through the maze?

Animal Dot-to-Dot

Join the dots to find one of my least favourite creatures.
Humans seem to find them a-mew-sing but I have no
idea why! I think they are **SCARY-SCARY-SCARY!**

Aldo's Mop Challenge

I enjoy watching my friend, Aldo the caretaker doing useful jobs around the school. He tells me lots of interesting things while he's working – and brings me yummy snacks, too!

Today Aldo's got a tricky word challenge for us. Read the first clue and change one letter in the word MOP to get the answer. Continue down in the same way but remember you can only change one letter each time, for each clue. If you do it right, you'll end up with the same word that you started with.

1. This is the sound you get when you're making popcorn. It's also a kind of music that just about everyone likes!

2. I often find one of these in my fruit, especially pieces of orange. I usually eat them but humans spit them out – strange . . .

3. When I'm thirsty, I take a _ _ _ from my water spout.

4. Without this, you couldn't kiss anyone.

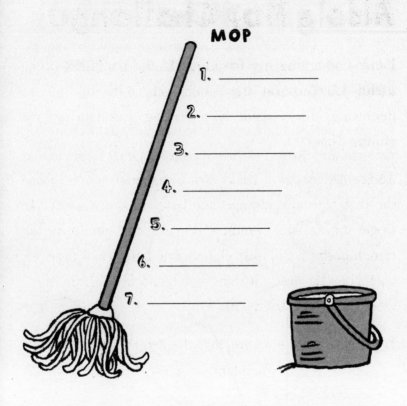

MOP

1. _____
2. _____
3. _____
4. _____
5. _____
6. _____
7. _____

5. When humans hold and stroke me, they sometimes put me on their _ _ _.

6. An essential item if you're looking for treasure – or just trying to find your way somewhere.

7. Change one letter and you should get MOP!

Design a Kite

Garth and A.J. once made a huge kite with a **LONG-LONG-LONG** tail on it. It was amazing!

Can you design a fantastic kite for a windy day? Draw patterns and use lots of bright colours. Don't forget to add a long tail!

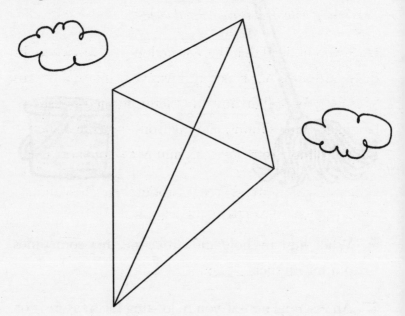

No 'E's today!

Once Mr E the supply teacher showed us this paragraph and asked us what was strange about it. Do you know?

> *This is an unusual paragraph. I'm curious how quickly you can find out what is so unusual about it. It looks so plain you would think nothing was wrong with it! In fact, nothing is wrong with it! It is not normal though.*

Have you noticed that there is no letter 'e' anywhere in the paragraph? Mr E said this was very unusual because 'e' is used more than any other letter in the English language. That's funny, coming from someone called Eddie Edonopolous! (We call him Mr E for short.)

Can you write some sentences about yourself without using the letter 'e'? Go on, give it a try!

Humphrey's Riddle Time

My good friend Garth once asked me a tricky, but fun, question called a riddle:

> *Everyone knows you must water a flower.*
> *Tip me over, I'll give it a shower.*

The answer is – a watering can!

I realised that I **REALLY-REALLY-REALLY** like solving riddles. And I've found some more for you – can you work out what they are? To help you, all the answers are mixed up below. You just need to choose the right one!

A TOWEL   **A SPONGE**

FOOTSTEPS   **FIRE**

PIANO   **A GLOVE**

A HOLE   **ENVELOPE**

1. What gets bigger, the more you take from it?

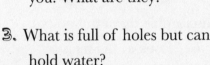

2. The more you take, the more you leave behind you. What are they?

3. What is full of holes but can hold water?

4. If you feed it, it will live. But if you give it water it will die. What is it?

5. This is a long word but it only contains one letter. What is it?

6. What has fingers but cannot use them?

7. What has many keys but no locks?

8. What gets wetter, the more it dries?

What's in the Lost Property?

You'd be amazed at what Mrs Wright, the PE teacher, has got in the lost property box!

All the items are mixed up – and now the letters are mixed up too. Can you unscramble them to find out what all the lost items are are? Look at the picture opposite to help you.

yek　　**cawth**　　**lalemurb**

_ _ _　　_ _ _ _ _　　_ _ _ _ _ _ _ _

lalb　　**nuxbloch**　　**hoes**

_ _ _ _　　_ _ _ _ _ _ _ _　　_ _ _ _

volge　　**kobo**　　**ripsed**

_ _ _ _ _　　_ _ _ _　　_ _ _ _ _ _

Match the Opposites

Mrs Brisbane once gave us a FUN-FUN-FUN opposites quiz – but, as usual, Raise-Your-Hand-Heidi forgot to raise her hand to say the answer!

Can you match up the pairs of opposites? You don't need to raise your hand – just draw lines between the right pairs.

up

cold

sad

slow

empty

tall

open

big

down

short

hot

closed

fast

small

happy

full

Humphrey's Spot the Difference

When Og and I were invited to Garth's party, we were both unsqueakably happy! Here are Garth and his little brother Andy. Garth is writing out clues for a **FUN-FUN-FUN** treasure hunt.

Can you find eight differences between the two pictures?

Humphrey's Super Spider Challenge

I can't understand why Stop-Giggling-Gail is so
SCARED-SCARED-SCARED of spiders!
Mrs Brisbane told us that they are very helpful creatures
who get rid of pests, like flies.

It made me think – how much do we really know about
spiders? So I found out lots of interesting things about
them and made a quiz for you in my little book.
Just answer **True** or **False!**

1. Spiders have six legs

2. A baby spider is called a spiderling.

3. A White Widow is a type of spider.

4. Some types of spiders live in lakes, ponds and streams.

5. A fear of spiders is called claustrophobia.

6. Spider's silk is incredibly strong.

7. A spider is a type of insect.

8. Spiders are covered in tiny hairs.

Humphrey's Holiday Jokes

As you know, dogs and cats are not my favourite animals. But I pawsitively love telling jokes about them!

Why is a dog so hot in the summer?

Because he wears a coat and pants!

What do cats like to eat on a hot summer day?

Mice cream.

Why do seagulls fly over the sea?

Well, if they flew over the bay, they'd be bagels! (bay gulls).

What do you find on a very small beach?

Micro-waves.

Which letter of the alphabet is the coolest?

Iced T.

My Favourite Season

A lot of people seem to love the summer because the weather is fine and they get to go on holiday. I like the summer because it's sunny and warm, and all my friends are happy!

What's your favourite season – Spring, Summer, Autumn or Winter? Draw a picture of your season and tell me why it's so **GREAT-GREAT-GREAT!**

My favourite season is _____

because _____

Summer Fruit Wordsearch

There's nothing I like more than munching on sweet, delicious summer fruits. Sometimes Aldo brings me a strawberry, or even a scrummy grape.

Can you find eight fabulous fruits in the wordsearch below? They might be up, down, across or diagonal.

**PINEAPPLE · MANGO · MELON · BLUEBERRY
STRAWBERRY · BANANA · GRAPE · RASPBERRY**

A	T	W	B	A	G	B	N	Y	P
I	M	E	L	O	N	D	R	S	I
P	P	U	G	P	G	R	W	G	N
L	I	N	R	L	E	G	O	W	E
R	A	S	P	B	E	R	R	Y	A
M	P	D	E	G	S	A	L	M	P
S	A	U	B	A	N	P	O	T	P
T	L	R	Y	S	P	E	Y	I	L
B	R	B	A	N	A	N	A	R	E
S	T	R	A	W	B	E	R	R	Y

Summery Odd One Out

Wow! I've been watching some of my friends pack their suitcases - humans take a LOT-LOT-LOT of things on holiday with them, don't they!!

Take a close look at all these holiday items. Can you circle one picture in each set of three that is the odd one out?

1.

A   B   C

2.

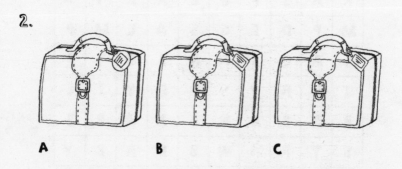

A   B   C

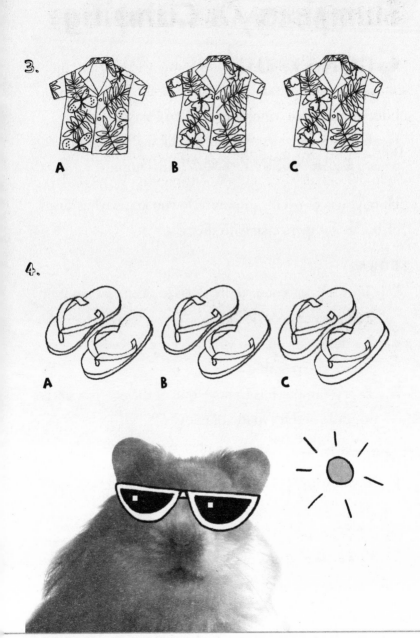

Humphrey's Camping Crossword

I discovered what 'camping' is when I stayed over at Heidi's house. It's sleeping outside all night in a tent – what a **GREAT-GREAT-GREAT** adventure!

Have you ever been camping? Do you know what kinds of things campers take with them?

DOWN

1. This is what you usually sleep in. You can zip it up and get really cosy! (8,3)
2. It's dark outside – so you need one of these to see where you're going.
3. Every camper has to have one of these – you sleep inside it and it's made of canvas.

ACROSS

1. If you want to cook something tasty and hot, you'll need one of these.
4. Most people put their tents up in a garden or _____.
5. Once your tent is up, you hammer these in around the edges to keep it secure.

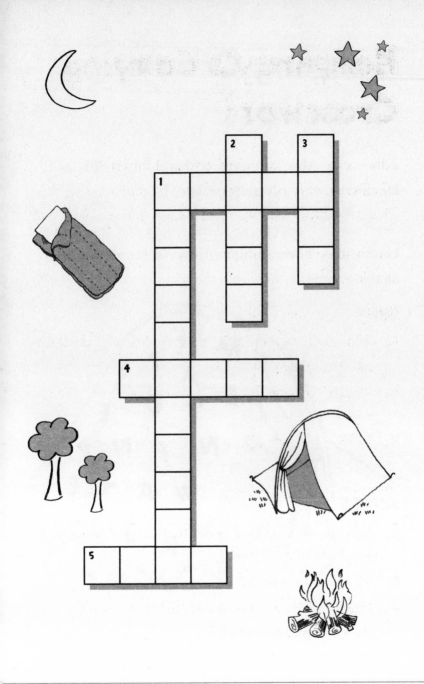

Camping Creepy Crawlies

Can you guess what creepy crawly things we found all around us on our camping night?

Find out by crossing out all the letters that appear twice on the tent. Then unscramble the remaining letters to find the word.

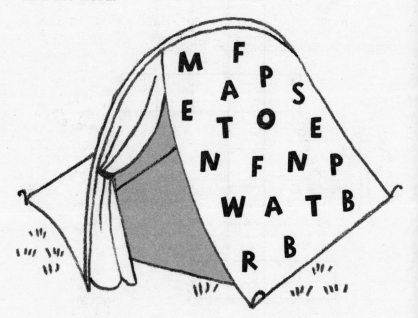

The word is _____

Spooky Shadow Dot-to-Dot

Did you know that you can make all kinds of weird shadow shapes in a tent, using your hand and a torch? The girls showed me how to do it on our camping night. They even terrified the boys with a horrible monster shadow!

Can you join the dots to find out which spooky shadow monster Stop-Giggling-Gail is making?

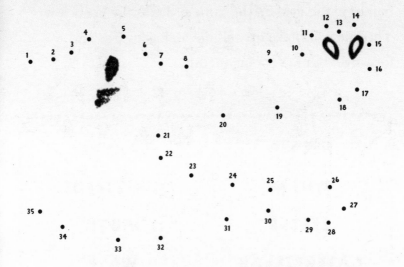

Now add some teeth!

Creepy Crawly Wordsnake

There seemed to be creepy crawlies all over the place on our camping adventure! I admit that I felt a little scared – even when the scary 'snake' turned out to be a garden hose!

Can you find the names of lots of creepy crawlies in this wordsnake?

Use a pencil to draw a continuous line through the names in the grid (in the same order as the list below). The line will snake up and down, backwards and forwards, but never diagonally.

SPIDER	EARWIG
WORM	CENTIPEDE
BEETLE	MOTH
CATERPILLAR	WASP

S	P	W	A	S
P	I	H	T	P
E	R	W	O	M
T	E	O	D	E
L	E	R	E	P
E	B	M	T	I
C	A	T	N	E
P	R	E	G	C
I	A	R	I	W
L	L	E	A	R

Humphrey's Summer Camp Rhyme Time

Being at Camp Happy Hollow was an un-fur-gettable adventure! I liked it so much that I wrote some camp rhymes in my little book when I got home. Can you fill in the missing rhyming words?

1. Summer camps are so much fun
   With games and sports,
   All in the _____ .

2. There's so much to do,
   Like swim or hike
   Grab a canoe
   Or ride a _____ _

3. I met a creature,
   Name of Jake,
   Was scared to find out
   Jake's a _____ _

4. Up a hill and way up high,
   Lovey the dove began to _____ .

5. Goldenrod was a little mouse
   Who lives outside,
   Not in a _____ .

6. With teachers and creatures,
   Girls and boys,
   Shouting and squeaking, there's lots
   Of _____ !

Dipper Dot-to-Dot

On our camping night, Golden Miranda pointed at the starry sky and showed us the 'Big Dipper'. It was unsqueakably hard to see at first, but I found out that it's a group of seven stars that you can join up with an imaginary line.

Can you find the Big Dipper by joining up the numbers 1–8? Then you can look for it if you ever go camping!

Finish the Postcard

When people go on holiday, they sometimes send postcards home to their friends and families. They have unsqueakably lovely photographs on one side and a space for a message on the other. I wish I could write one!

Would you like to finish this postcard message? Just fill in whatever word you like! Perhaps you could write it to me?

Dear _____

I'm having a _____ time here

at _____ . I'm with

_____ and we're

staying in a _____ .

We're having lots of fun _____

_____ and _____

_____ . The weather

is really _____ and the

food is _____ .

Wish you were here!

_____

(your name)

New Names Quiz

The summer holidays are coming to an end, but there's always more to look forward to. Like the beginning of the new school year at Longfellow School!

After the summer holidays I was unsqueakably surprised to find Room 26 full of new children. I learnt lots of new names that day. Can you fill in the missing words from their names?

1. Slow _ _ _ _ -Simon

2. _ _ _ _ _ _ Paul

3. _ _ _ _ Joey

4. _ _ _ _ _ _ _ Holly

5. _ _ _ _ _ _ _ Rosie

6. Hurry- _ _ -Harry

7. Be- _ _ _ _ _ _ Kelsey

ROLLING

CAREFUL

DOWN

UP

SMALL

HELPFUL

JUST

Hope you all had 'furry' happy holidays! See you next summer.

Your pal – Humphrey

Answers

p. 1 Summer's here! RELAX!

p. 2-3 Rocking Reports Water Skills, Loud Noise Making, Splashing, Being Very Green, Wheel Spinning, Hamster Ball Rolling, Squeaking, Helping Your Friends.

p. 4 Humphrey's Noises 1. Og 2. Gail 3. School Clock 4. School Bell 5. School Gate 6. Humphrey 7. Aldo's Trolley

p. 7 Og's Pond Maze Og will eat **5** crickets

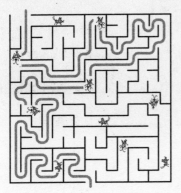

p. 7 Finish the Camp Song 1. Ears 2. Hole 3. Boat 4. Greenl 5. Mountain 6. Ocean

V	E	H	G	M	O	I	N	G
O	C	G	N	I	K	I	H	S
L	K	A	R	C	H	E	R	Y
L	S	O	N	M	M	G	C	B
E	O	H	S	O	L	I	N	G
Y	K	V	R	C	E	B	A	R
B	S	W	I	M	M	I	N	G
A	R	C	N	E	L	S	N	C
L	N	O	G	B	A	V	L	G
L	L	A	B	T	F	O	S	R

p. 12 **Humphrey's Secret Message** Lovey was a **dove**

p. 14 **Humphrey's Secret Message** The scary haunter is called the **Howler**

p. 16 **Which Snake is Jake?** Jake is a **Garter** Snake

p. 18–19 **Humphrey's Secret Code** I love surprise parties!

p. 21 **Humphrey's Word Wheel** Let's go round again!

p. 22–23 **Fur or Feathers?** The six birds are the kiwi, the quail, the albatross, the heron, the kestrel and the falcon. The other six are furry mammals – like Humphrey!)

p. 24–25 **Humphrey's Trivia Bee** 1. Giant Squid 2. Six 3. Kids 4. Purple 5. Captain Hook. 6. Three horns 7. The horse chestnut tree 8. Six sides. 9. Some kinds of grasshopper 10. Pinocchio 11. They are muscles on the arms 12. All of them are hamsters, but not c) French!

p. 24-25 **Hot or Cold?** Camel – HOT, Kangaroo – HOT, Walrus – COLD, Polar Bear – COLD, Ostrich – HOT, Penguin – COLD, Lizard – HOT, Hyena – HOT

p. 28-29 **Humphrey's Ice-cream Wordsnake**

V	A	N	I	U	T
O	C	O	I	N	O
I	A	H	L	O	C
I	T	C	A	C	A
S	T	R	N	A	N
P	W	A	A	B	E
E	R	O	C	O	I
Y	R	G	N	F	F
M	T	T	A	M	E
I	N	O	F	F	E

p. 30 **Summer Fair Sayings** Frog, Speak, One, Cool

p. 34-35 **Humphrey's Seaside Word Grid**

1. SWIM
2. BEACH
3. BOAT
4. CRAB
5. ROCKPOOL

p. 36-37 **Party Odd One Out** 1. C 2. A 3. B 4. A

p. 39 **Humphrey's Park Wordsearch**

M	O	N	K	E	Y	B	A	R	S
S	P	S	E	E	S	A	W	O	M
W	A	F	W	K	U	L	G	U	W
I	U	N	C	I	A	W	N	N	I
N	E	C	D	G	K	B	E	D	G
G	E	B	T	P	F	D	K	A	P
D	N	M	E	E	I	W	H	B	M
B	S	P	U	L	J	T	I	O	B
I	D	N	S	G	A	W	M	U	U
O	U	T	M	W	K	S	K	T	A

p. 42-43 **Summer Picture Puzzler**

p. 44-45 **Humphrey's Secret Code** School's out for summer!

p. 46-47 **Humphrey Around the World** 1. New York 2. London 3. Tokyo
4. Sydney 5. Paris

p. 48 **Aki's Rockin' Maze**

p. 50-51 **Aldo's Mop Challenge** POP - PIP - SIP - LIP - LAP - MAP - MOP

p. 54-55 **Humphrey's Riddle Time** 1. A hole 2. Footsteps 3. A sponge
4. Fire 5. Envelope 6. A glove 7. A piano 8. A towel

p. 60-61 **Humphrey's Riddle Time** 1. Andy is not wearing glasses. 2. Garth
is writing two paper clues, not one. 3. Andy's shirt has a different pattern. 4. The
volcano in the picture is now a tree. 5. The dinosaur in the picture has more spots.
6. Og looks unhappy. 7. There is a now a little sleeping hut in Humphrey's cage 8.
There is a spider hanging down above Andy's head.

p. 62 **Humphrey's Super Spider Challenge** 1. False – they have eight legs.
2. True. 3 . False – but a Black Widow is definitely a spider! 4. True. 5. False – a
fear of spiders is called arachnophobia! 6. True. 7. False – a spider is an arachnid.
All insects have six legs. 8. True.

p. 65 **Humphrey's Park Wordsearch**

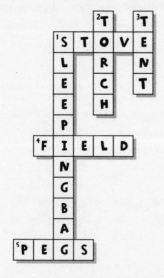

A	T	W	B	A	G	B	N	Y	P
I	M	E	L	O	N	D	R	S	I
P	P	U	G	P	G	R	W	G	N
L	I	N	R	L	E	G	O	W	E
R	A	S	P	B	E	R	R	Y	A
M	P	D	E	G	S	A	L	M	P
S	A	U	B	A	N	P	O	T	P
T	L	R	Y	S	P	E	Y	I	L
B	R	B	A	N	A	N	A	R	E
S	T	R	A	W	B	E	R	R	Y

p. 66–68 **Summery Odd One Out** 1. B 2. A 3. A 4. C

p. 68–69 **Humphrey's Camping Crossword**

```
              ²T      ³T
      ¹S T O  V  E
        L     R     N
        E     C     T
        E     H
        P
  ⁴F I  E  L  D
        N
        G
        B
        A
  ⁵P E  G  S
```

p. 70 **Camping Creepy Crawlies** Worms

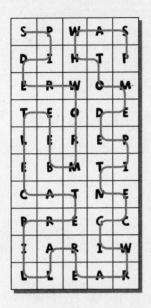

p. 75 **Humphrey's Summer Camp Rhyme Time** 1. Sun 2. Bike 3. Snake
4. Fly 5. House 6. Noise.

Humphrey and his friends have been hard at work making a brand new FUN–FUN–FUN website just for you!

Play Humphrey's exciting new game, share your pet pictures, find fun crafts and activities, read Humphrey's very own diary and discover all the latest news from your favourite furry friend at:

www.funwithhumphrey.com